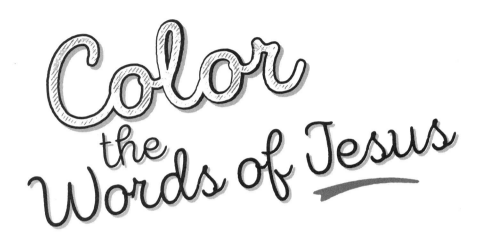

Color
the
Words of Jesus

Artwork by Marie Michaels

HARVEST HOUSE PUBLISHERS
EUGENE, OREGON

Scripture quotations are taken from…

The Holy Bible, New International Version®, NIV®. Copyright © 1973, 1978, 1984, 2011 by Biblica, Inc.® Used by permission. All rights reserved worldwide.

The New King James Version®. Copyright © 1982 by Thomas Nelson, Inc. Used by permission. All rights reserved.

The New American Standard Bible®, © 1960, 1962, 1963, 1968, 1971, 1972, 1973, 1975, 1977, 1995 by The Lockman Foundation. Used by permission. (www.Lockman.org)

Cover by Katie Brady Design

COLOR THE BIBLE is a registered trademark of The Hawkins Children's LLC. Harvest House Publishers, Inc., is the exclusive licensee of the federally registered trademark COLOR THE BIBLE.

COLOR THE WORDS OF JESUS

Copyright © 2017 Dugan Design Group
Published by Harvest House Publishers
Eugene, Oregon 97402
www.harvesthousepublishers.com

ISBN 978-0-7369-6947-5 (pbk.)

Printed in the United States of America

17 18 19 20 21 22 23 24 25 / ML-CD / 10 9 8 7 6 5 4 3 2 1

A Good Place to Begin

This coloring book is for artists of all ages and talents, and that means you! Let your creative spirit free, choose any color you like, and make each beautiful image your own. There are no rules except to have fun.

Enjoy the process. Feel free to use colored pencils, pens, watercolors, markers, and crayons—or any combination—to add color and texture to each design. Notice that all the pictures are printed on just one side of the paper. To keep colors from bleeding through to the next page, simply slip an extra piece of paper underneath the page you're working on. When finished, you might like to remove the page from the book, trim it to size, and frame your artwork for all to see.

Most importantly, have fun with the process. Enjoy experimenting with contrasting colors or different shades of the same color. Try lighter hues for a softer look or layer and blend your colors for even more options. Allow some white space or saturate the entire piece with rich vibrant color, depending on your mood. Let your worries go, relax in the moment, and allow your creative spirit to lead the way!

Blessed are the pure in Heart, for they shall see God.

MATTHEW 5:8

Seek first His Kingdom AND HIS RIGHTEOUSNESS. and all these things will be given to you as well.

MATTHEW 6:33

Ask and it will be given to you; Seek and you will find; Knock and the door will be opened to you.

MATTHEW 7:7

Follow Me.

MATTHEW 9:9

Come to Me all you who are weary and burdened, and I will give you Rest.

MATTHEW 11:28

TAKE COURAGE! IT IS I. DON'T BE AFRAID.

MATTHEW 14:27

Where two
or three gather
in my name,
there am
I with them.

MATTHEW 18:20

THE SON OF MAN
did not come to be served,
but to serve, and to give his life
as a ransom for many.

MATTHEW 20:28

Well Done

GOOD AND FAITHFUL SERVANT!

MATTHEW 25:21

MAY *Your Will* BE DONE.

MATTHEW 26:42

I am
with you
ALWAYS
to the
very end
of the
age.

MATTHEW 28:20

YOUR SINS ARE FORGIVEN.

LUKE 5:20

Give, and it will be given to you.

LUKE 6:38

LUKE 7:50

FATHER, *Forgive* THEM.

LUKE 23:34

PEACE BE WITH YOU.

LUKE 24:36

You must be BORN AGAIN.

JOHN 3:7

It is I; don't be Afraid.

JOHN 6:20-21

I AM THE BREAD OF LIFE.

JOHN 6:35

JOHN 8:12

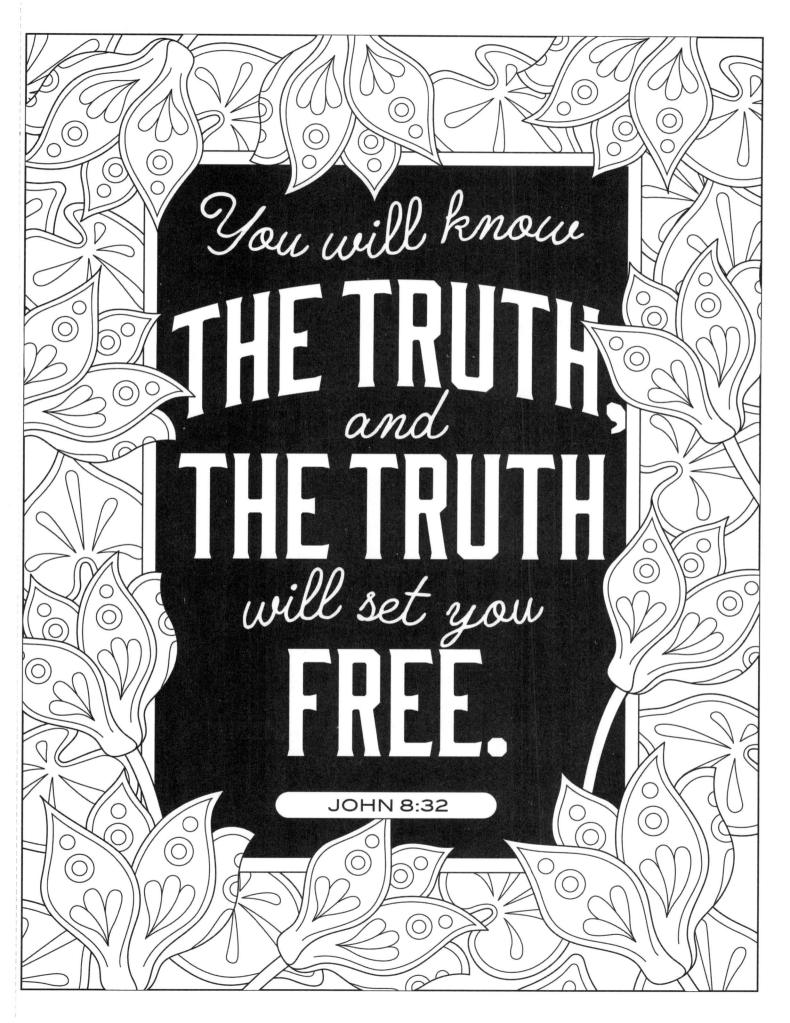

I AM THE Good Shepherd.

JOHN 10:11

I am the Resurrection and the Life.

JOHN 11:25

Love one another.

JOHN 13:34

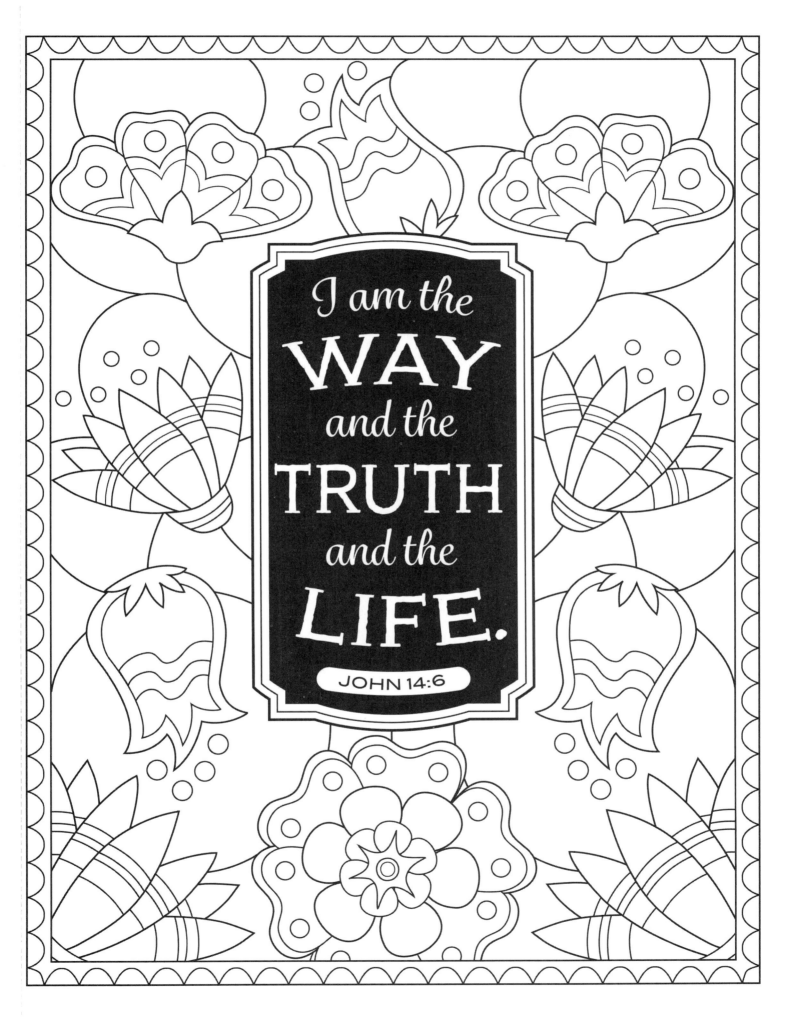

Do not let your hearts be troubled and do not be afraid.

John 14:27

I am the Vine; YOU ARE THE BRANCHES.

JOHN 15:5

I HAVE Overcome the World.

JOHN 16:33

I AM THE
FIRST
AND THE
LAST.

REVELATION 1:17

Marie Michaels represents the combined work of three artists from Dugan Design Group in Minneapolis, Minnesota: Nicole Wallace, Chris Dugan, and Terry Dugan. Their primary creative work is book cover and book interior design, increasingly focused on original content through illustration, photography, and digital media.

We'd love to see your creations!
Share your finished projects on social media with the hashtag

#colorthebible

We'll be looking for your artwork!

For information on more
Harvest House coloring books for adults, please visit
www.harvesthousepublishers.com